This book is to teach you to play gin rummy. I think I'm the best (at least one of the best) players in the world. I win 75% of all the games I play. No brag—just fact!

If you want to challenge me on the internet, I'll tell you how to reach me. If you want to meet me in person, I'll tell you how to find me. But for now, I want to teach you to play winning gin rummy because I love the game and I love the challenge. If you read this book, you'll become a worthy opponent. Oh, you won't beat me, but you'll beat most of the other players in the world.

Unless of course they, too, read my book.

Play Gin To Win

Strategies for:
Internet
Tournaments
Recreation

by

Charley Killebrew

Swan Publishing
New York ✶ Texas ✶ California

Author: Charley Killebrew
Editor: Pete Billac
Layout Artist: Sharon Davis
Cover Design: Sharon Davis & Tiffany Davidson
Photographer: Manny Chan

Copyright @ May 1999
Charley Killebrew and Swan Publishing
Library of Congress Catalog Card #99-62671
ISBN# 0-943629-40-3

PLAY GIN TO WIN, is available in quantity discounts through Swan Publishing, 126 Live Oak, Alvin, TX 77511. (281) 388-2547 or Fax (281) 585-3738.

Printed in the United States of America.

DEDICATION

This book is dedicated to all the "old pros" who helped shape my character, and to the new computer generation of *online* players who entertain me in the twilight of my gin rummy days.

The "old pros" are: Isidore Jansburg, jeweler; Sonny Martini, theater owner/landlord; Larry Yeager, my favorite *bookie* and school chum; Paul "Bananas" Stalone, longshoreman; Stan Schrieber, comedian; and Aaron Schneider, entrepreneur and close friend (who knows me so well I can't intimidate him).

And to the World Play gin players: PBanta, Gloalert, Sportsmom, emeyer, ohdearpen, Ajpotts, Jolene, and the inexplicable, irascible, Flairman99, without whose inspiration this would not have been written.

INTRODUCTION

After playing gin on the internet for several months, it became increasingly apparent to me that there are a lot of players who **do not know** how to play gin correctly. That is the reason why I am writing this manual.

This book is not intended to help the experts, most of whom you could not, *under any circumstances*, give advice; they are too smart for that. I thank God every day for sending me those "experts." Without them I would have never made so much money playing gin rummy.

The beginners and the players who never have taken the time or effort to understand and fully comprehend the intricacies of gin rummy will improve their play immensely by reading this book. They will enjoy the game more and so will their opponents.

Believe me. It's no fun to play a *neophyte* or an uninformed player. There is no challenge. Therefore, no sense of gratification in defeating a person that you know is not a worthy opponent. It's like winning the heavyweight championship of the world with a baseball bat.

Unless you're a total dunce, you will achieve some measure of success after reading this book and then *studying* it. Wishing you many victories over those opponents, who, in the past, have been kicking your butt.

TABLE OF CONTENTS

A BRIEF BACKGROUND OF THE GAME

Gin Rummy was invented in New York in 1909 by a gentleman named Elwood T. Baker as an improvement on *Knock Rummy*. He called it "gin" because the parent game was called "rum," another alcoholic drink. Gin Rummy is *the* most popular two-handed card game in the world, and is not only a wonderful pastime but and excellent way of keeping one's mind exercised.

Since the advent of card playing on the internet, this particular game will become even more popular, enabling a person to play "live" with people all over the world, and also to participate in tournaments and establish their own credibility as an excellent gin rummy player among their fellow competitors.

You can't always find a player in person, but you can always find a gin game on *the net*. Other card games are also available on the internet; bridge, hearts, spades and cribbage. But if you want to play bridge, spades, or hearts on the net you need four players. And if one of those players decides to quit in the middle of a game the whole game falls apart until you can get another player to take their place.

Sometimes it takes a long time to get a foursome, and even longer to find a *replacement* player when one of your players drops out. So gin rummy is the way to go! Learn more about the intricacies of the game and develop into a serious contender.

That is what brought about the writing of this book. Playing on the "net" made me realize that a lot of people know how to play gin but do not know how to play *well*. By reading this information I have accumulated over a period of more than fifty years and practicing what I teach, you will raise the level of your play and become more competitive, maybe even an "expert," like me!

If your level of play is already high, you will still derive some tips from this book that will help some aspect of your game. If any of this happens—and it will—I will have achieved my goal; to help many to become better players and enjoy the challenges of this wonderful game.

DA' ROOLS

If you already know the rules of Gin Rummy, pass up this chapter and go on to learning how to become an EXPERT at playing this game. Skip ahead to chapter one.

On the other hand, if you're not certain, read this part. I hate wasting print.

It's pretty simple. Two people, one standard deck of fifty-two cards. The dealer alternately gives ten cards face down and turns the twenty-first card face up next to the remainder of the deck (now called the stock), thirty-one cards of which twenty-nine are playable. You don't play the last two cards. Don't ask me why, this wasn't my idea.

The value of the cards are: face value, ace being one, and all face cards are ten.

The non-dealer has the option to take or refuse the *upcard.* If the non-dealer passes, the dealer has the option of taking or passing the *upcard.* If neither accept it the non-dealer then draws the top card from the stock and discards from his hand.

You never have more than ten cards in your hand after completing your turn. You may only pick up the top card from the discard pile and you may not look past the top card to see what has been discarded. Don't worry about this rule while playing on the *internet*. You couldn't even if you wanted to.

The object of the game is to form matched sets, consisting of three or four of a kind (groups) or of sequences (runs) of three or more cards of consecutive rank in the same suit.

A player may *knock* in any turn, after having drawn and before discarding, if the value of the unmatched cards (*deadwood*) in his hand is ten points or less.

You don't *have* to *knock* but it's the smart thing to do. That's *my* rule, not the official rule. Having *knocked*, he discards one card face down and lays his hand, arranged in matched sets and unmatched cards. The opponent then spreads his hand, playing his matched sets, if any, lays off whatever cards he has that match the *knocker's* matched sets. The point values of the two players unmatched cards are then compared, and the result of the hand is scored. If the *knocker's* count is less than his opponent's, he wins the hand, and the difference in points is scored to his credit.

If the opponent *ties* or has less *deadwood* count, he has *undercut* you and scores twenty-five points plus the difference in the count, if any.

If all your cards are matched and you have no *deadwood* you have ginned. You receive twenty-five points for gin plus all the point value in *deadwood* from your opponent and he cannot lay off any cards on your melds.

When playing in person, you can make your own rules governing the number of points you want to play to, who deals first, whether winner or loser deals and whether to deal the eleventh card to your opponent or to turn it face up. It's your game, you play it the way you want to.

However, when playing on the *internet*, the rules are established and you have to abide by them. You can choose between *Oklahoma, Hollywood, Oklahoma/Hollywood,* or just straight gin. The games are played to 100 points and the winner deals!

In *Oklahoma Gin,* the first *upcard* determines the minimum count on which a player may *knock*. If that *upcard* is a face card or a ten, 10 you may *knock* with 10 points as usual. If it is a spot card, you need that number or less. If it's an ace, you must gin. If both players agree (if the *upcard* is a spade) scores for that particular hand are doubled in value.

Hollywood Gin is a method of scoring gin rummy so that, in effect, three games are played simultaneously. A player's *first* win is entered only in the scoring column of game 1; his *second* win is entered again in game 1 and *also* in game 2; his *third* and subsequent wins go into all three game columns. The three games are terminated and scored separately. When a game ends, no further scores are entered into that game. When the third game ends, a new series is begun.

Before you begin playing, you and your opponent have the option of playing *Straight* gin, *Oklahoma* gin, *Hollywood* gin, or *Oklahoma/Hollywood* gin, and with that spade option. There are lot's of choices to *cream* your opponents.

Chapter

Name of the Game

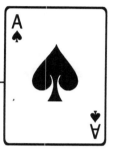

Whether you are playing gin rummy for fun and relaxation, or playing for money (or in a tournament), it is always infinitely more fun to win than to lose. In order to give yourself the advantage over your opponent you must usually have the *percentages* on your side. I say "usually" because luck plays such an important part in the game that it can overcome percentages—-but not always, and rarely with regularity. LUCK is when opportunity meets preparation. So, prepare by reading what I have to tell you.

However, if luck is spread out evenly then you definitely want the percentages on *your* side and you'll win the majority of your games.

Again, this book will get those odds heavily in *your* favor. But, if your **opponent** reads this book and you don't, the odds will be stacked against you!

There are probably ten million (more or

less) "best" gin rummy players in the world, all of whom have, basically, the same knowledge of the game. The outcome of their play is mostly determined by *mental discipline* and after that, to a large extent, luck.

Luck of the draw enables anyone with a minimum sense of card playing skills to win at gin, but *mental discipline* affords the better players *continued* success. Because of luck, a one-eyed, retarded chimpanzee playing against an expert could win a game but in the long run the expert, taking the advantage of knowing percentages, will surely come out victorious.

Do **not** expect to win every game you play, even though that should be your ultimate goal. That's wishful thinking. All you have to do to be a *winner,* is to win 51% of your games.

It's ludicrous to think you can win *every* game of anything. And though winning 51% of the time is certainly not a large margin of success, if you are playing for money you will come out ahead.

And, while you won't always be playing for money, you still want to win for the satisfaction of being considered the better player. The *margin* of winning matters not; winning does. My personal goal is to win 70% of the games I play. Since I began playing on the internet, I have won 74% of my games overall and 71% in tournament play.

You will find, after playing for many years, that cards will often run in *cycles*, with one player winning game after game then having the cards change for the benefit of the other player and they, in turn, will win a disproportionate amount of games. That's just the way it is.

This will happen more often playing with real cards as opposed to playing on the *internet* using a computer. So do not be discouraged if you find yourself losing to an opponent you know you can usually beat, knowing full well that you are playing well and not making mistakes. Keep playing as well as you can, go with the percentages, and pray for some luck!

Chapter

The Upcard

This is what I recommend to help you to have an advantage over your opponents.

Beginning with the *upcard* (the card that is turned face up after the players are dealt their ten cards) if you have first choice and the *upcard* matches two or more cards in your hand you MUST take it.

If you do not and your opponent takes it, you will then have two or more cards in your hand that you cannot dispose of until you find out which way that *upcard* is being used. That makes sense, doesn't it?

And even then, only one of them will be a *safe* discard. An exception to this rule: if your hand is so good that you only need a card or two to *knock* or if you have no convenient discard— if all your cards are in potential groups or sequences (runs), then you should pass.

Illustration #1

You hold:

3♠, 3♥, 4♣, 4♦, 7♠,
8♣, 10♠, Q♥, K♠,
K♦, the *upcard* is the
eight of spades,
you MUST take this
card. For two rea-
sons: it affords you
the use of four addi-

Illustration #1
Your Hand

tional cards, the 6 and 9 of spades, and the
other two eights, and you discard the queen,
which would have been your normal initial discard; and if your opponent *picks* the upcard, you
are stuck with the 7 of spades, 8 of clubs, and 10
of spades! That is far too many cards to hold and
at least one that they certainly need, possibly
two.

Illustration #2
Your Hand

Illustration #2

You hold:

A♠, 2♠, 3♥, 3♣, 6♠,
7♣, 10♠, J♣, Q♦,
K♥, and the upcard
is the queen of
clubs. Again, you
must take that card

and discard the king (and hope your opponent doesn't pick it up or if they do it is to be used in a sequence, not a group). This gives you four additional cards to use. The 10 of clubs, the king of clubs plus the other two queens.

If you had allowed your opponent to have that card, you would be stuck with thirty points in unplayable cards. Study this a moment and see what I'm telling you.

And in the event that the small end of the hand develops, you can always dump those *biggies,* starting with the jack of clubs if your opponent picked the king you discarded, or the queen of diamonds, which will still give you a chance to make a run by catching the king or the 10 of clubs. Don't forget that 50% of your cards come from the deck. Don't expect to get too much help from your opponent.

Illustration #3

You hold:

A♠, 2♠, 2♥, 5♣, 6♣, 6♥, 9♥, 9♠, 10♠, 10♥ and the upcard is the 7 of hearts. Looks very nice in your hand, but if you pick it up, chances

Illustration #3
Your Hand

are you will not get the 7 of clubs or the 8 of hearts from your opponent.

Besides, you can knock by catching only two out of twelve available cards. Also, the correct way to play this hand is if you catch a 9 you discard a 10 and vice versa. If you catch a jack or 8 that makes a sequence, discard the 10 that is not in the run; that's safer than breaking up the 5, 6, 6 combo, unless it has been shown that the 10 may be a "hot" card, then discard the 9.

Then, if you catch a card to the 5, 6, 6 combo you should knock unless it has taken too long to reach this point, but it's not a bad hand to try and gin, and your opponent will not make a lot if *they* knock.

However, if the same upcard is there and matches two or more cards in your hand and your opponent has the first choice and does *not* take the card, DO NOT pick up that card. Because, first, you are *speculating* and your opponent will not give you anything to go with it and you'll have to draw a matching card yourself (a 50% chance). And secondly, it provides you with two or more safe discards.

Exception: if your hand is so bad that you only have one or two pair or only two cards in a sequence and that upcard will give you an opportunity to use an additional four cards, then take it.

Illustration #4
Your Hand

Illustration #4
You hold:
3♠, 4♣, 5♥, 6♠, 8♣, 9♥, 10♠, J♦, K♣, K♠ and the upcard is the 8 of hearts or 9 of spades, or 10 of diamonds, you might want to speculate. Any one of these cards offers you the use of *four* additional cards, and at the present time you can only use the other two kings and nothing else!

Incidentally, when you have a hand like this, and you will, play a game within the game, trying to hold this particular hand to as little a *loss* as possible.

Remember, you cannot win ALL the hands, but you must try to give up as *little* as you can. Sometimes you will actually win this hand and it will be very gratifying.

Let's say you picked up the upcard, the 8 of hearts and discarded the jack of diamonds. Next card, you get the king, discarding the 10 of spades. One card later, you draw the 5 of spades, so discard the 4 of clubs.

Next two draws give you a run 8, 9, 10 of

hearts and another run 5, 6, 7 of spades, and now you've got a five-way option to gin or knock for three and you've only had four turns not counting the upcard. Lucky? You bet! But luck plays an awful big part in this game.

Don't forget that your opponent has the same opportunities as you. So when they have first choice, it is possible that they are picking up the card in self-defense and are not necessarily making a "spread" with it. Try not to give them anything that is closely related to that card as long as you possibly can, or until they give an indication how they are using it

Illustration #5
You hold:
2♥, 2♠, 4♠, 4♣, 7♥, 8♣, 8♦, 10♦, J♠, K♣ and the upcard is the 8 of hearts, a card you needed. Your opponent takes this card. You, of course, do not give an 8 and certainly not the 7 of

Illustration #5
Your Hand

hearts, and if the 9 of hearts shows up in your hand or in the discard pile, you know they are speculating.

They drew first, so they discard first and you mimic whatever they throw away whenever possible or as close to that card as you can.

This brings us to the subject of "bait" cards. This is what makes the game even more fun. When you want to *entice* (trick) your opponent into discarding a specific card you need, you discard the *same value* card but in *another* suit they will throw you the card you need.

For example, you throw away a 5 of any suit because you need the 5 of clubs and you hope by discarding this 5 your opponent will feel safe and throw you the 5 you need. This works—sometimes.

Now, if your opponent *picks up* that "bait" 5 you are throwing away, this is the time to watch more closely to determine whether your opponent is using the 5 you threw away in a *group* or in a *sequence.* If the evidence is such that he is *not* using it in a sequence, you will never get the 5 of clubs that you need.

More of the intricate parts of this game. Sometimes the "fish" take the bait and never get caught. And the sooner you can put out this "bait" the better because if you wait too long to throw out that "bait" card, it just might match up with something in their hand. Yeah, a fun game!

Also be aware that your opponent might

"bait" you. The majority of the time your safest discard will be to match his bait. A *safer* discard (notice I said "safer" and not "safe") is one that "touches" on your opponent's discard and one that you have a duplicate of in your hand.

For instance, they throw away a 7 of diamonds and you have another 7 in your hand along with a 6 of diamonds, plus another 6 that you are using in a sequence. The 6 may very well be the safest discard when choosing between the two. Think about all the consequences before making any discard. ALL of your plays are critical. Want to win at gin MOST of the time? Begin to think this way.

Reading Opponents

Be aware of "body language" when playing someone in person, face-to-face, as opposed to playing *online* with the computer. Unlike playing online, you have the opportunity to observe your opponent's gestures, grimaces, hands shaking, etc.

Some "expert" card players will put every card in their hand, shift the cards around, and then discard so you will never know if they kept the card or not. If they pick up your discard you know they can use it (unless they are trying to throw you off), which is not a good strategy because it wastes a turn and the number of turns you get are very important.

Watching *closely* when a player puts a card in their hand is important. Some players, upon making a spread, will move those cards to one end of the hand and you will know when they have been successful. After they have moved three groups of cards to that specific part of their hand, you certainly don't want to knock!

Also, if you pay attention to where the discards originate in the opponents hand you can sometimes tell if they have higher cards than the one discarded. Most players will keep their cards in numerical order, either low to high, or high to low. After a few hands you will begin to see the trend and can take advantage of this knowledge.

However, the more astute players never divulge this type of information simply by not revealing where the cards come from or by rearranging their cards from hand to hand and you can never figure them out. (None of this aforementioned material will be of any use in computerized games).

I have found through some misfortune, that one of the disadvantages of computer play is that you cannot rearrange your hand while holding eleven cards (after drawing and before discarding) because occasionally, when moving a card with your *cursor*, it will inadvertently be discarded.

That's a *bummer*! There's nothing worse than to patiently wait for a key card and then throw it away while trying to reposition it.

Which brings me to the benefits of keeping

one's hand positioned where you can see clearly which cards you need and can use, and which ones are useless or belong in your opponent's hand. In order to keep your mind clear so that it can function on more important matters of the game, keep your hand in neat order so that it becomes very clear as to which cards you need.

Illustration #6
Your Hand

Illustration #6
You hold:
2♥, 2♠, 3♥, 5♦, 5♣, 6♦, 8♥, 8♦, 10♥, 10♠. This hand should be arranged like: 2♠, 2♥, 3♥, 5♣, 5♦, 6♦, 8♦, 8♥, 10♥, 10♠.

The 2 and 3 of hearts should be touching so that you know you need an ace or 4 of hearts. The 5 and 6 of diamonds should be touching so that you know you need a 4

Illustration #6
Arrange Your Hand Like So

or 7 of diamonds, which would tie in with the 8 which is aligned with 6 as is the 8 of hearts with the 10 of hearts. You can discern, with little difficulty, which cards you need from the start. Actually, this is a very nice hand even though it starts out with no spreads.

If an ace presented itself in the first or second draw you should take it and discard the 10 of spades. This would give you the opportunity to *knock* after catching any two of seven available cards and if you decided to go for gin, you could throw back the ace that was discarded.

Don't try to get cute and spread your cards out haphazardly so as to confuse your opponent; you will only handicap yourself. **Concentrate** on the cards you need. MAKE them show up! There is that element of *mind over matter* and it works in gin rummy, as does mental telepathy. And if you do not believe me, concentrate and try it! You will be surprised and rewarded.

With a little practice and some confidence you can make your opponent *give* you a card and they will be surprised they did it! That's more of the fun in this game. Isn't it great?

On rare occasions you will be dealt a hand with *two spreads* and a good combination of other cards that will place you in good stead for that particular hand. Be aware that your opponent may have the same good fortune that you have! Do not assume that you have plenty of time to gin.

Illustration #7
My Perfect Hand

Illustration #7
My Perfect Hand:

I once had the *perfect hand*, 6, 7, 8 of clubs, diamonds, and spades, which gave me nine ways to gin; you can't get more than that. My tenth card was a jack. My opponent had picked up a jack so I thought I was in excellent shape to win the hand by ginning or by undercutting him if he *knocked.* He did indeed *knock*, but my jack did not play and I lost the best hand you can have.

There is no moral to this story. I did the absolute correct thing by playing the hand as I did—to gin. The percentages were definitely on my side but you can lose even with a perfect hand. Yeah, a fun game.

Chapter

Knock!

This Is the Most Important Information in this Book! Please Read it Carefully.

The object of gin rummy is NOT to gin, but to *knock* ASAP! You need to limit your opponent to as few draws as possible so that they cannot develop their hand. Sometimes only one draw is necessary to change the hand from a thirty-point loss to a thirty-point win.

Illustration #8
You hold:
2♠, 2♥, 3♥, 3♠,
4♦, 5♦, 6♦, Q♣,
Q♥, K♥.

Illustration #8
Your Hand

Your opponent holds: 4♠, 5♠, 6♠, 8♥, 9♥, 10♥, 10♣, J♣, K♣, K♦.

You draw the jack of hearts to make two spreads with the twos/threes combos in two suits which is very tempting to play to gin, but being an astute player, you *knock* for ten. If you had *discarded* the

Illustration #8
Your Opponents Hand

queen of clubs your opponent would have ginned and scored 35 points, but instead you scored 30!

Knock as soon as possible, ALWAYS! Of course there are exceptions. Aren't there always?

If you have five or six gin cards that you know are available and your opponent will unknowingly and willingly give them to you, then you have a *good opportunity* to go for gin. Even when you are far behind, that's no excuse for trying to gin. That is the number one mistake made by most gin players.

I have won thousands upon thousands of gin games and have never ginned even one hand during those games. Just recently I won a tournament of six rounds of play, 100 points per game, and never, **never** ginned once!

Sure, I've been undercut so many times that it doesn't even faze me any more because I know I've made the *correct play* and in the long run. I (usually) win. On some occasions, through no fault of your own, you will have to play to gin.

Illustration #9

You hold: 4, 5, 6 of spades, 7♣, 8♣, 8♥, and 10, J, Q, K of diamonds.

Illustration #9
Your Hand

The **best** chance you have of winning the hand is to complete the 7, 8, 8, combination which will gin this hand.

If you draw a card that you know is one your opponent needs, you may have to break that combination in order to hold their card, or you may *take the chance* that it will not gin them. You can't win them all!

If you *do* hold the opponent's card, you will probably not gin the hand. The majority of times in that circumstance, I give my opponent the card and hope he doesn't gin or *knock.*

The *score* of the game at the time also enters into the decision. The closer your opponent is to going out, the more *defensive* you must play. Sometimes the cards are not going your way and you need some outside help.

On those rare occasions, your only option is to resort to *mental telepathy* and faith in the "card gods" to help you. Concentrate on the necessary cards and make them come to you!

You may be skeptical about this statement, but *try* it some time and you will be delightfully surprised!

I've noticed on the *internet* (where you will meet some very bad players) that a lot of players fall in love with all those "pictures!" Then they "romance" their cards. They get so carried away with how grand those kings, queens, and jacks look that they collect as many as they can. Forget about *knocking!* Play these gorgeous things to gin!

I believe that a lot of players like face cards because they learned to play *500 Rummy* before they learned to play gin. In *500 Rummy* (a typical child's game) it is ideal to have all those pictures because that's how to score the most points. They forget that those same points count in their **opponent's** hand too! When they are caught collecting all those *pretties* and they don't meld, they lose a lot of points.

Get a deck of cards and lay them out as you go through this book. This way, you'll be able to "see" what I recommend.

Chapter

Speculating

Do not pick up a face card to speculate!

An exception exists here, of course. That is if it **matches** two or more cards in your hand and you do not have anything else in your hand from which to draw. But, you *still* want to dump them as soon as you get some a smaller pair, or an ace or deuce to swap for them.

Conversely, pertaining to the *upcard*, if it is an ace, deuce, or trey and you have two or three face cards or nines or tens, take this opportunity to *pick* the small card and *dump* one of the big ones. It may be one that your opponent needs, but you were going to give it to them anyway.

It usually benefits you to speculate with small cards. Even if you don't make a spread with them, you need them to *knock* and if you get caught with them they only count for a few points. They are VALUABLE.

Again, do not ever think that you can win *every* hand. Most of the time you will recognize a pitiful hand where you can only use two or three cards in the whole deck. Don't panic! It's one of those time when you have no choice in the matter; the "card gods" are not smiling on you—this time. This is the time to escape with as few *losing points* as you can.

Take every card three or under you can get your hands on and **START DUMPING!** Your goal is to try to hold the loss to a small number. "Fight, fight, then run away. Live to gin another day!"

On some occasions you will surprise yourself and actually win with a very poor hand. You can make a poor hand into a *knocking* hand with as few as four or five draws.

Illustration #10
Your Hand

Illustration #10
You hold:
A♦, 3♥, 4♣, 5♦, 6♥, 7♠, 9♠, J♥, Q♣, K♦, With this holding, the **only** card you can use is the 8 of spades in the middle of the 7 and 9, known as an "elbow

card". (That's when you put the card only part-way into the hand between the cards that it goes with and then push it down the rest of the way with your elbow.)

That says, sarcastically to your opponent, that they just gave you a card in the middle. Op-ponents laugh at this move but secretly *hate it.* Oh, this game is so much fun. Actually, this move helps you determine whether your oppo-nent will be your friend, regular gin partner, or just someone to play gin with when the ones you care for are not available.

You don't have the luxury of making this move on the *internet.* But, you can draw a jack that goes with either the queen or the king, and draw a 5, 6 or 7 that connects either the 5-6 or the 6-7 together and in the next two draws com-plete those two combinations and *knock* for eight! All this in only four draws.

> Don't despair if a hand looks totally hopeless. NEVER give up on any hand. Minor miracles happen all the time in gin.

Sometimes, when you have one of these pitiful hands, your opponent's hand is just as bad. Or they could have a great hand and never draw a card to it. Think how many times this has happened to you. All you needed was one or two cards to knock or gin and they never showed up.

There are thirty cards in that deck to be drawn from (including the *upcard* and discounting the last two cards) which are never played; go with those odds, or at least *understand* them.

Occasionally, the ten cards you need will be in the bottom twelve of the deck and the same misfortune can happen to your opponent.

Since the object of the game is to *knock* and not to gin, usually you need to make two spreads and have your *deadwood* (cards that do not play in a group or sequence) totaling ten points or less. Try to make *runs* (sequences) instead of groups because *runs* can have any number of cards. But *groups* can have only four.

Illustration #11

You hold:
2♠, 3♥, 4♣, 7♠s, 7♥, 7♦, 10♠, 10♦, 10♣, Q♠. You have available a 7 or a 10 to

Illustration #11
Your Hand

get in order to knock for 9 points.

If your hand was like Illustration #12 (2♠, 3♥, 4♣, 6♠, 7♠, 8♠, 10♥, J♥, Q♥, K♠) you have

Illustration #12
Your Hand

the 5 and 9 of spades, plus the 9 and king of hearts to catch; **twice** as many chances! And if you choose _not_ to _knock,_ you can add on and on to a sequence, but there's only four in a _group_.

See my point, and why I favor a run over a group?

At the beginning of every hand, try to assemble four _deadwood_ cards that total ten or under, unless your hand is so good that it is not necessary. All you need is two spreads and that _deadwood_ and you're ready to _knock_.

If your opponent discards an ace, deuce or trey **pounce on it** and dump some picture or 9 or 10 you know that you will never use in that particular hand.

Concentrate on the cards you need to make your two spreads and knock.

Every time you pick up a *small card* it is one more card your opponent will have to *think* about. Besides, you can always give it back later if the situation changes. Conversely, look to get back a card like that from your opponent if they are doing the same thing you are doing, and plan to use it in your hand.

Many players are affected by an *undercut* and it sometimes makes them angry. Getting angry only takes a player out of their winning strategy. This is a fun game; enjoy playing for the sake of playing . . . and winning, of course!

Never let being *undercut* upset you. It happens to very good players a lot more often than it happens to the people who try to gin all the time.

I was undercut three times in a tournament game (playing to 100 points) and still won the game and never ginned!

My opponent would never *knock* for fear of being *undercut,* and would have won the game if he had just *knocked* once but he was having so much fun and success undercutting me, he thought that was the surest way to success. **WRONG!**

On an *internet* game I played an

Oklahoma/Hollywood game and won all three games by shutout and never ginned! Three different hands I only scored one point! My opponent asked me how I could do that, and I replied, "Smoke and mirrors." Also told him I had an extra deck of cards that I could get what I needed from. And that by using my other computer I could see his hand. I think he wanted to believe me.

Occasionally you will lose to someone who will never *knock* because they want that 25-point bonus that goes with the gin and the undercut (sounds like the right strategy).

Again, the odds and percentages are OVERWHELMINGLY in your favor if you knock ASAP. Remember this and you'll win a lot at Gin Rummy.

In some hands you will find yourself in a position where you cannot possibly *knock.* In these instances, you play to *gin,* or you play to get to a *tie.* Try to be as certain as possible that your opponent cannot *knock* or gin and catch you holding almost all of his cards.

Illustration #13

You hold: an ace, deuce, trey of spades, ten, jack, queen of clubs and a live 9 plus three cards you know to be ones your opponent needs (5 of

Illustration #13
Your Hand

clubs, 6 of hearts and the 8 of diamonds). Your opponent has picked up a 5 of spades, 6 of clubs, and the 8 of spades. There is almost **no way** for you to win this hand, but you can play for a tie by holding all the cards you know to be his. And if he *knocks* you lay them off.

You may have to even break up your ace-deuce-trey combo, discarding the safest one first. Remember you cannot win all the hands but if you must lose one, make it minimal.

Chapter
Defense! Defense!

You hear the word "defense" during many football and basketball games. It works for winning gin rummy also. Do not give your opponent a "suspect" card after they have shown that they can possibly use it. If the *upcard* or one of your discards is picked up, say for instance the 7 of hearts, do not give them another 7, nor the 6 or 8 of hearts. This, I know, is not necessary information for good gin players.

However, sooner or later in the course of playing out the hand, you are holding what you suspect is a "live" card, one that you cannot use but has not shown up as yet during the play of the hand; a 5, for example and no fives have been played yet and you hold no other 5 in your hand.

You may be better off to give them the *known* card (one you *suspect* they need) possibly giving them four of a kind, rather than a new card which will make a new spread.

Sometimes you will be pleasantly fooled and they did not need the "hot" card you had been keeping.

Early in the hand, your opponent picks up a card that touches on or is one like you have in your hand. Say they pick the jack of clubs and you are holding a jack of hearts and the queen of clubs, both cards having the possibility of going with the jack of clubs.

All the remainder of your cards are essential to your hand's success and you certainly do not want to part with them. *Test* your opponent immediately, discarding the card that you feel is the safest. If he can use it, chances are the other card will be a safe discard.

With this holding, always give the card of the same *rank* or *value* that was picked up. In this case it would be the jack. If you give the queen and he also picks it up, it could be jacks and queens or it could be a run. If the jack is taken, then the queen is usually a safe discard.

Chapter

Percentages

I'm not going to bore you with a bunch of numbers showing percentages. *Most* of what I tell you is only COMMON SENSE, which I have found to be the biggest misnomer in the world. Why it isn't common, I'll never know. *Humans!* Who can explain their minds?

Gin Rummy is simplistic. In the majority of hands, the *cards* dictate the play of the hand. You cannot make something out of what you do not hold; you have to work with what you are dealt.

Also, the type of game you're playing dictates your strategy. If you're playing *Oklahoma,* you must keep a card or combination of cards (deadwood) that will allow you to knock.

If the *upcard* is a 2, 3 or 4 you have to play the hand accordingly. Recently, I was dealt a hand that had three kings, three queens, two aces and two deuces and the *upcard* was a 5.

My *deadwood* totaled six and I could not catch a queen, king, ace, deuce nor the trey which matched an ace/deuce combo and I lost the hand. **Cards dictate the play of the hand,** and in this case, I was victimized by a beautiful hand.

Later, playing the same person, I was dealt Ace, 2, and 3 of spades, three kings, the 10 of diamonds, jack of diamonds, jack of clubs and an off 9. The *upcard* was a king (which I took) and discarded the 9, hoping my opponent would not need it and then give me the 9 of diamonds when *it* showed up.

The 9 was not picked up and I was sure I would gin the hand when my opponent then discarded a queen. We each had about seven or eight draws at which time my opponent *knocked* with all the small cards I had passed. Should I have broken up the ten/jack combo when I'm faced with certain gin?

Yes! When my opponent picked up the first ace I discarded. I should not have given him anymore small cards. But, sometimes you make up your mind to "dance with who brung you" (what you were dealt) and you have to pay the piper. Depends on how badly you want to win.

If you really don't care about winning, stop reading my book this very instant. PLAY stupid and STAY stupid!

Remembering Discards

Other than *knocking* first, the most important aspect of the game is to remember ALL the
discards. It's not difficult to do.

The majority of hands only last through a
couple of draws by each player. The faster you
can *knock,* the better off you are! (I'm not suffer-
ing from total *Alzheimers,* I know I've said this
before, but it's an important point to remember;
it's how to win at Gin.)

However, there will be hands that you cannot catch the cards you need early and your
deadwood never totals ten or less. (Also, different strategy prevails in *Oklahoma Gin,* which will
be discussed later.)

So it is imperative that you remember all
the cards that have been discarded. If you do not
want to be that dedicated to playing gin correctly,
you can forget about ever becoming an expert
player and just depend on luck in order to sur-

vive.

It's not that difficult to do. Here's how I do it. Mentally divide the deck into three sections: ace through four, five through nine, and ten through king. Since no one wants to get caught with cards worth lots of points, face cards are usually discarded early.

Of course your opponent is also aware of this, so holding two kings, queens or jacks early can be an asset. However, if they do not show up early, you will want to consider dumping them ASAP.

Another situation is (if you are far behind in the score) do NOT dump high cards in the hope you can knock early and catch your opponent with some pictures that haven't developed! But if you *are* far ahead, don't let them catch you with that "royal family of bastard cards" or they will soon catch up.

It is usually easy to remember the face cards that have been played. Kings are the "end of the line"; nothing plays on a king but a queen. However, some confusion may arise if aces are also played as high cards (some players use aces high and low.)

Illustration #14

Illustration #14: Q♠, K♠, as where the ace is played as a high card.

There is also a *finality* on the low end with no card played on an ace except a deuce unless you're playing "around the corner."

Illustration #15

You hold: K♥, A♥, 2♥, 3♥. These options are available on the *internet* game, and some players like this format. I don't!

I recommend that you avoid these options and place the ace as *low* only and no "around-the-corner" bullshit! Another option is "spades doubled." Do not get sucked into playing that crap, either. Just play the game without messing it up with a dozen little changes.

Illustration #15
Possible Format

Play it as it was meant to be played.

Those versions are all *amateur games* that allow players with lesser skills to compete by winning some "cheap" games.

"Never play another man's game." My father taught me that at a very early age. If you are going to compete to win, make the opponent play the game *you're* best at or more comfortable with. Most tournaments are played *Oklahoma /Hollywood,* 100 to 150 points per game, without spades doubled and aces are low only.

If you are more comfortable playing just plain gin, then play your game, unless you just want to be a gracious loser that day. If they don't like it, let them go play someone else. You can always find another sucker, er, ah, player.

Internet tournaments are usually *Oklahoma* to 100 points, which is fast and doesn't favor the superior player because the game is too short. But it gives everyone a chance to win and that's also fun and challenging.

REMEMBERING DISCARDS, *cont.*

At the other end of the spectrum, ace-four is also easy to keep an account of what has been played. If at all possible, you never give away any ace, 2 or 3. That may be just the card that enables your opponent to decrease his *deadwood* low enough to *knock—and win!*

The most difficult to remember are the

cards 5 through 9 and are also the best cards with which to work. You can make longer runs and more switches and at the same time prevent your opponent from getting his necessary cards.

But with enough diligent practice you can remember **all** the cards, **all** the time! This separates *the men from the boys*.

Remember this, please. There are only fifty-two cards in the deck. They never change. They have been the same ever since I started playing gin fifty-odd years ago, and they will be the same forever. You get ten, your opponent gets ten, one is face-up and there are twenty-nine to draw from and the last two are not playable, nor is the last discard when only two cards are left.

A helpful hint: after every hand, make a conscious effort to clear your mind; erase everything from previous hands, and play very deliberate—but not slow. You can almost *feel* the mental freedom when starting a new hand with nothing left over from the last hand stored in your brain.

When you get your hand and arrange it, you usually have a very distinct goal with two or three possibilities for making groups or runs

(runs preferably, but not necessary to success). Sometimes you are fortunate to already have a spread about every other hand. So does your opponent.

Do not *speculate* by picking up a card to make a pair, or to make two cards in a se- quence. If the *upcard* is an ace, deuce, or trey, grab it if you have some high cards to dump. If you have for example, the 6 of hearts, 6 of spades and 7 of spades and the *upcard* is the 7 of hearts, *then* speculate because it gives you so many options. It gives you the use of eight avail- able cards.

And *especially* if your opponent has indi- cated that they did not want it, or if it was dis- carded. You can always—*safely*—give it back later.

Chapter

Oklahoma Strategy

You are regulated to *knocking* by the value of the *upcard*. If the *upcard* is a 5, you cannot knock until the *deadwood* in your hand is five points or less. If it's a 2, then you must have two points or less. If it is an ace, then you must gin.

This dictates a little different strategy in the play of the hand. Since there are twenty cards with a value of ten, and another twelve cards with a value of seven to nine, it doesn't affect the game too terribly much.

However, when the *up* card is an ace (you must gin), deuce, or trey, you must alter your play accordingly. When playing to gin, try to go with the cards that are hidden (those in your hand on the deal and those you draw from the deck, rather than your opponents discards) as much as possible so your opponent has *no earthly idea* what you have or need.

If your hand is *very* bad, you will have to

speculate from the very beginning. Try to go with *runs* rather than *groups* because you are going to need one group of four or a run of four in order to accomplish gin.

Occasionally you can gin with two runs and no groups, and it is possible to gin with three groups, but it is harder. If you find yourself with three or more of your opponent's cards, play for the tie.

You may even break up your own spread if you need some safe discards. Only do that with small cards in case you're not successful, and if your opponent gins, you want to have small cards that will not count too much.

The hardest hand to play is with a deuce turned up. Just remember to keep an ace or deuce in your hand at all times so you can *knock*. Otherwise, you must play the hand to gin.

Whenever possible, grab that *up* card when it is a 2 or 3 to keep your opponent from having that advantage. When the *upcard* is a 2, 3, 4, or 5, it usually means you will need three spreads in order to knock. You can make two spreads and have two aces and two deuces (six points) and cannot knock. On hands that are in this category, try to go with runs instead of groups, but don't force it.

Two runs allow you four cards to catch; two

groups only give you two cards to catch and that's a huge percentage advantage. Catch any one of those cards and you can *knock*. Catch two and you are in good shape to do whatever you want.

Chapter	10 ♠ ♠ ♠ ♠ ♠ ♠ ♥ ♥ ♥ ♥ ♥ ♥ 01

Decisions—Decisions

When holding certain combinations that are perplexing, remember to use *common sense* and keep the percentages on your side.

Illustration #16

You hold: 5♣, 6♦, 6♠, and 7♣. All the other cards in your hand are pairs or already made into spreads. You must discard one of these four cards. Which one?

The 6 of clubs is the only one that will complete the run with the 5 and 7 of clubs, but either outstanding 6 will make a group with the two you already hold. If you discard a 6 and your opponent picks it up to make sixes, not only

Illustration #16
Your Hand

are you stuck holding the other 6, but you NOW have the 5 and 7 of clubs and they are totally worthless. Your obvious discard is the 7 or the 5.

Either of these should be determined by what your opponent has picked up, or which card is the safest. When in doubt always discard the *higher* card—the 7.

Two points could be very important at the end of the game, the difference in your opponent going out or having to play another hand, giving you still another chance to win.

Another holding that is sometimes confusing is for:

Illustration #17

You hold: 7♣, 7♦, 8♦, 9♥, and 9♠.

You are at a point where you must discard one of these cards. If you discard a 9 and it is not picked up, you have a chance to get the 9 of diamonds which will make you a run, but you are left

Illustration #17
Your Hand

with two useless cards in your hand.

If you throw the 8 you have the opportunity of making two groups. The 8 is the *liveliest* card, since you are already holding two sevens and two nines. Either discard offers you the same number of cards possible to use.

Discarding a 9 first, you can use the 6 of diamonds, the other two sevens and the 9 of diamonds. If the 9 is picked up by the opponent, you probably only have three cards available, plus you're stuck with the other 9 which may also be their card.

By discarding the 8, you have the two sevens and the two nines and you are not left holding a *live* card.

However, if it is being used as a *run* and not a *group* by your opponent, you may only have two cards to catch, the case 7 and the case 9. Most of the time if your opponent picks the 8 you will get a 7 or a 9 as a discard in return.

Chapter
Strive for Superiority

If you suddenly have this overwhelming desire to become a "super player" you must be prepared to play EVERY hand to its fullest potential. You have to be mentally alert to every nuance of the game. You have to comprehend every possibility of your opponent's hand. Your hand is an open book to you. It's the easy one to play. You know the possibilities and percentages of completing your spreads.

What you need to do is to VISUALIZE all the *possibilities and percentages* of your opponent's hand. If the hand is over within the initial three or four draws there is not much strategy or mental activity involved, and a lot of hands end that early (hopefully yours!). It's nice to catch a few of those "no-brainers."

It's not until after each player has drawn and discarded four or five times that you start to have any idea about what possibilities exist in both hands.

Let's say your opponent has picked up the *upcard* or one of your early discards, say the 8 of hearts. You have to discern all the possibilities that entails.

A *run* possibility covers all cards from the 5 to the jack of hearts, and a *group* involves the other outstanding eights.

Suspect cards are eliminated through the play of the hand as various cards appear that will give you the information you need to find out how that 8 is being used.

If you have the 7 or 9 of hearts plus another 8 and no 6 or 10 of hearts has shown, and you need to discard one of those three, you discard a 7 or 9 if either of those have been played in another suit or if you are holding either in your hand.

Your *safest* discard is the 8. If you discard the 7 or 9 and they pick it up you won't know if they have a heart run or eights and nines, or eights and sevens, depending on your discard.

Never give a *suspect* card to an opponent until you absolutely must! You can very easily draw a card that matches it and discard another combination of your own that you were holding, especially if it has a *safe* card in it.

Don't "fall in love" with your cards and think that you must hold them just because you had them from the deal. Be very flexible with all your holdings; none of them are sacred.

Sometimes, you may have to take a card off your run or throw away one of a group of four in order NOT to give your opponent a card you know he can use, especially if you think it will gin him.

Always be prepared to play for a draw or lose the hand giving up only a small count. **No one wins all the hands, remember?** But it's the winners who give up the *fewest points* on losing hands.

♥♣♦♠ ♥♣♦♠ ♥♣♦♠ ♥♣♦♠

The most aggravating people to play are the ones who pick up every discard that matches ANYTHING in their hand. They will pick up cards that make pairs or to make a two-card run. The absolute worse ones will pick up a *king* if they have a jack in that suit! I have seen it.

The worst part is, I have *lost games* to these *aliens from an unknown planet!* But, people who play like that will always lose over the long haul. You simply cannot make five or six spreads with ten cards, and that's what their strategy seems to indicate.

The **smartest** way to play, and I'll say this again and again, is to **KNOCK as soon as you can!** When you play against speculators, it is devastating to their plans; they haven't had time to collect all the cards that will give them the most possibilities to make their four or five spreads.

When you *speculate*, you are passing up the opportunity to draw the very card you need to make a spread.

After you've established the fact to your opponent that you knock at every first opportunity, you need to *play* a hand or two (ones that have a good possibility to gin), thereby throwing some doubt as to how you play.

If you *undercut* the ones often enough, you know, the ones who try to gin every time, they reason that they must then resort to *your game* and *knock* in order to win.

Yes, it's an absolute **impossibility** to make three spreads with one containing four cards faster than a player can make two spreads and a handful of small cards. Oh, I very well know it does happen; it's happened to me over 50,000 times. But if those same people play me for more than a few games I will beat them.

And there are always those who will invariably gripe and crumble about "those *cowardly* players" who always knock and are afraid to go for gin. Don't let it affect you, let it affect *them!* Grumble, grumble, grumble, let's win and have fun doing it.

Against very good players (the ones who play the game as I play it) you have to maintain discipline and never give in to hunches or impulses. I know this is useless information to give to *female* players because their intuition is so much more acute than mine is, or ever will be.

Because you know you are playing an excellent player, you have to be that much more disciplined and mentally alert. And if the cards are running against you, do not despair. They will turn around to your way again—they always do.

And remember again, **never, NEVER** give up on *any* hand, no matter how bad it looks. I've seen it happen far too many times. You have a miserable hand and your opponent has picked up three discards and you don't have but a couple of pairs. Hang in there.

If they haven't *knocked* yet they're probably speculating or going for gin which may give you just enough draws to win or hold the hand to a small loss. Besides, what else can you do?

You can't concede the hand. You can't quit and walk out. Sometimes, with some truly terrible hands, that seems like the best idea. But, **never give up on a hand!**

MORE WINNING TACTICS

Play deliberately. Do not play fast and above all, do not play slow. Don't *pounce* on the *upcard* or discards, but maintain the same pace whether you have just gotten a middle card in a five-card sequence or a totally useless card. Or even worse, one of your opponents cards.

Try to not spend too much time *analyzing* a discard, unless you're deliberately trying to throw off your opponent.

When drawing or discarding, try to maintain the same pace. Try to have your thinking already finished and know what cards you need so you won't give any clues to your opponent as to whether you *almost* needed that last discard.

Since your plan is to *knock* early every time, make sure you keep the necessary count in your *deadwood*. It's a terrible feeling to sit there with two spreads and hold eleven points in deadwood and draw, and draw, and draw . . . and all the while you're watching your opponent stuffing more and more cards in his hand.

Chapter

Courtesy

In playing on the *internet,* you meet all types of players. Most of them are courteous, friendly people who just want to relax and have some fun. There are a few, however, who are arrogant, obnoxious boors and do not try to hide that aspect of their pitiful lives.

They act like playing with them is everybody's goal in life whereas most people would rather ignore them. Such is life.

My advice is just bypass them the same as a like kind you meet in everyday business. I favor a fun life and if you are around those who are no fun, duck them like a drunk uncle at a church party. You will neither change nor embarrass them, just get away from them.

You *internet* players, be polite to one another and enjoy the competition. If someone is extremely lucky and continually gins or *knocks* on the second or third draw allow them to enjoy their luck; it could be *me* you're playing. Or worse, my friend Aaron Schneider. Why I like that guy is beyond me.

If you do find a lucky person, they probably have earned it and the *card gods* are paying off. Just don't *quit* in the middle of a game with no explanation to your opponent as to why you are leaving. If you get knocked *off line* (which happens too frequently to me) get back as soon as possible and try to reach your opponent and explain to them what happened.

Don't *grouse* about how fortunate they were to win all those "no-brainers." Your turn will come and you will reap the benefits of those early gins and *knocks*. It isn't your fault that you caught all your cards early and they didn't catch theirs.

I usually make it a practice, that if I gin on the first or second card to start a new game, I offer to restart the game so as not to take advantage of a cheap win. When someone wins a game, tell that person, "good game" or "nice play" etc.

In a tournament, by all means be gracious when losing and congratulate your opponent and wish them further success in the tournament. You should *pull* for the player who beat you to win the tourney; makes you look not-so-bad.

More importantly, be a gracious *winner*, and thank everyone for playing well, trying their best and you will hopefully see them in another tournament. And thank the people who run the tournaments; theirs is a tougher job than you realize.

The nastiest cut of all is the player who, after winning the initial game the two of you have played, quits and makes some snide remark concerning your lack of ability or of their superiority. They have a win against you and they're not going to let you get even, or ahead. Don't be a coward. Don't be a hit-and-run artist. If you win, give your opponent an opportunity to play again no matter how badly you think they play.

Chapter

The Card Gods

The card *gods* I speak of now and then, are the ones in charge of who gets which cards and whatever they draw subsequently. If you play your cards well and make no mistakes, the card gods will smile on you and continue to give you good cards.

However, if you are guilty of making *dumb* plays too often, you will make them unhappy and they will no longer give you those good cards. Poor play and poor decisions anger the card gods and it takes a lot of excellent play to get them back on your side. My advice: play intelligently!

And, mental telepathy can play a large part of which cards you get from your opponent when playing face to face. If you are good at it, you can also do it *online*.

For instance, whenever you need a specific card and you sense your opponent is holding it, and they are trying to make a decision as to what to discard, you can help them make that decision by *concentrating* on the card you need.

Don't think of more than one card at a time, that will only weaken your power. Sometimes you can actually "feel" the card coming to you. If these thoughts are alien to you, you just don't have an affinity for the game.

Try to get in *harmony* with the cards. Then they will become your friends, along with the card gods. Sounds goofy? Maybe? But try it.

There is also a phenomenon that occurs infrequently when a card you *thought* you were holding is no longer in your hand. You look, and it's gone! I call this "molecular migration." It has departed your hand and is now residing elsewhere.

I have always suspected the *card gods* are largely responsible for this arcane behavior.

CARD SENSE

Some people have it and some don't. Certain players have the ability to "see" what the opponent is holding after only a few cards have been picked up, by what cards have been discarded, and by what cards are left to be played.

On some occasions, however, you can be

completely fooled by very good players who specialize in *chicanery*. I sometimes do that to throw off an opponent who is adept at *reading* players.

MENTAL TOUGHNESS

As I have grown older, I find it more and more difficult to remain mentally tough over a long period of time. After playing for three of four hours I begin to experience mental laxity and no longer care if I win or lose.

When *you* reach your saturation point and you began to feel "mentally tired," quit playing and rest for a while; you can always go back to playing after you're refreshed.

Go outside, walk around the block, get some fresh air, go to the bathroom, tell your opponent that you need a break; they might appreciate a break also. A break can do wonders for the mind.

PHYSICAL FITNESS

It also helps to be physically fit when engaging in mental activities. I work out three or four times a week and it helps me immensely when competing in long tournaments. Brisk walking, working out with light weights, eating properly; all these things add up to making you not only a better card player but a better person.

LEVELS OF PLAY

I have two distinct levels of play and I suggest you do the same; I'll tell you what I mean.

When playing for relaxation, I play mostly offense, using defense only when I get to serious play or when it's absolutely necessary. And when luck is with you, you can *win, win, win,* with very little brain work. It's very relaxing.

But don't play that way if you really want to win, only if you don't care if your opponent gets to win and *feels* good for having finally beaten you. You really should let them win once in a while. Otherwise they'll have bad thoughts about you, insult your mother or tell you to *fornicate elsewhere.*

At the *competitive* level, it is totally different. You have to concentrate on *every* card, *every* angle, and every nuance of your opponent. You have to think of every possibility that a card can be used for when it's picked up by your opponent. It's more of a *defensive* than an *offensive* game.

You almost NEVER give a card that can possibly be used by your opponent except when it gives you no way out by holding it. And I've stated this before, you cannot win every hand.

When you realize you are going to lose a hand, hold the loss to a minimum. Check the score, and know how many points you are holding in deadwood. If possible, throw some potentially *good* cards away if you think you're going to lose the hand so your opponent won't *win the game* on *that* hand, and hope for a better hand the next deal. Lose the battle, do not lose the war!

I repeat, maybe a fourth or fifth time, *never give up on any hand!* Keep searching for ways to *win* a hand. Sometimes little miracles happen.

Chapter
Cheating
(Don't Read This)

Playing on the *internet* does not afford much opportunity for **cheating**. About the only thing you can do is to "snatch" the *upcard* so fast that your opponent hasn't had a chance to see it before it's gone! Then when they ask what the card was, you say, "I don't remember." You'll make very few friends with stunts like that.

Playing in person is another story altogether. There are so many ways to cheat I could write a whole chapter on it. And, here it is.

While shuffling, watch the cards and notice where they are located in the deck. Obviously you will not be able to see too many of them, but all you need is to know where a few of them are.

For instance, you see the jack of spades and the 3 of diamonds at the bottom of the deck, you shuffle a couple of times and they are still going to be in approximately the same location.

Then, you offer the deck to be cut, paying close attention to the *depth* of the cut. Now, you know in which part of the deck they will be located. If in the *upper* part (the top twenty cards), they will be in either your hand or your opponent's hand. That gives you the benefit of ten percent of the cards already in play.

Additionally, if you watch closely when the deck is being cut, sometimes you can detect which card is on the bottom of the deck and will not be in the play of that hand. Armed with that modicum of knowledge, you know not to try to make a spread that involves that particular card.

For instance, if the bottom card is the 5 of clubs and you have the 4 and 6 of clubs, you know that's an impossible sequence to complete. And if you're holding two fives your chances of making fives has been cut in half. So when you're cutting the deck make sure your opponent cannot garner that information, and conversely, if you're in the mood for a little nastiness, you can take a peek yourself and gain that advantage.

Another method of cheating is to draw two cards at the same time and later discard two cards simultaneously. With a little practice it's not a difficult maneuver to pull off. Double your pleasure, double your chances of winning. If you get caught you claim it was an innocent mistake, you certainly didn't intend to do that, the cards just stuck together.

I don't advocate doing that, but if it's done *to* you, be wary of your opponent. Know what I mean?

Discarding is another matter. If you make it a habit of straightening out the discards by picking up the whole pile and arranging them so you can't see the prior discards, you tip off your opponent on ways that you play.

But, you can have the *two* discards in your hand as you place them on the pile and squeeze them together. Your opponent isn't allowed to move the top card to see what's underneath because that would be cheating!

And, if your opponent *knocks* while you're holding eleven cards, call for a misdeal (be sure you only do this when it's *their* deal).

Occasionally, when someone is holding a bad hand, they will draw two cards and then, *after* you draw, will announce that there is a misdeal because they just discovered they have eleven cards. If you have a *good* hand and they were the dealer, tell them to forfeit their next draw and just discard. Of course, if *you* have a bad hand, throw it in immediately.

Still, another sneaky thing to do is *lay down*

false spreads. You only do this when your opponent knocks or gins. He is so happy to have finally won a hand that he sometimes *forgets to
check* to see that all of your cards actually *play.*
Don't forget he is looking at your cards *upside
down* and sometimes sequences with a missing
card look perfectly natural. I know fathers' who
do that with their young kids.

Don't try it with groups, unless it's twos and
threes or eights and nines and put the "impost-
ers" in the middle, *partially* hidden. Sometimes
you can get by with a four between two aces if
you only expose the top of the four.

If you are beating someone badly, and
they're almost "blind" from being so distraught,
you can play off cards on their melds when they
knock and announce they have been caught
"speeding" or that they need to "get it fixed," that
you've just undercut them.

They will sometimes be so angry that they
won't even notice they've been hoodwinked! If
you get caught at this scam you can always say
you were just kidding, and give them their points.

A real amateur way of cheating is to drop a
card on the floor (remembering the card you've
dropped) and play a few hands without it. It will
give you the advantage of knowing not to play for
that particular card and your opponent may need

it and will wonder why it just never shows up.

If possible, drop it *closer to them* than your-self. That way, when it's discovered missing, you can always blame them. Sometimes, when an opponent has *knocked* or ginned, and you're holding a lot of deadwood, or if you have played off some cards on him (assuming he has *knock-ed*), you may take this opportunity to drop a card, preferably a big one. Then they will not get enough count to win the game. If you have three spreads, don't try this ploy.

Occasionally you can get away with an-nouncing "gin," especially when it decides a game and you have been trouncing your oppo-nent. You can lay down a false spread, usually an ace, deuce and trey in either red suit or either black suit with one card not being the correct suit. Please don't try this with red and black mixed together! Once I did this with a four card run, ace through four, spades with a club thrown in there, saying "gin!".

My opponent looked at my false spread and told me I didn't have gin. I replied with a smile, "I didn't say 'gin', I said 'ten'," (which ace through four adds up to in deadwood). I do this only with close friends for the fun of it. I pull this on Aaron now and then, just to hear him com-plain. I love him, but he truly *is* a complainer, yet fun to play against in gin.

He thinks he's as good as me—but he's *not*. He *is* good though, and getting better all the time. I'll give him that. (Well, I have to. He'll read the book first.)

Why cheat? **You really shouldn't.** But in the gambler's world I grew up in, it was a large part of the game and all of them did it—to an extent. And in reality, you don't get away with too much if you are playing with astute card players.

It's the ones who *think* they're good that you can fool the most, the *hot shots* who feel certain that no one can beat them. They are, in fact, the easiest ones to dupe. And I formerly took great delight in doing just that.

But these were not friends; they were the enemy, and I would go to any lengths to separate them from their money, just as they were trying to do to me. I certainly didn't invent cheating, I only tried to perfect it.

GLOSSARY OF TERMS

Bait—cards that are discarded to make your opponent think that any card of the same denomination is a *safe* card to give to you.

Body Language—enthusiasm in drawing and discarding, facial expressions, stiffness of body, edginess, excessive chatter, altering of cards in hand, etc.

Card Sense—an acute awareness of how and where the cards fit into the scheme of things when playing out a hand.

Deadwood—all the cards in the hand that do not form a group or a run.

Group—three or four cards of the same denomination.

Live Card—one of the four in that denomination that has not shown itself in the play of the present hand.

Molecular Migration—the ability of an inanimate object to travel from one place to another on its own, totally undetected.

Pat Hand—a hand that has no cards that are not necessary to the hand. They do not all play, but are not discarded until a spread is made with their counterparts.

Safe Card—the card that you know to be 90% sure that your opponent cannot use.

Sequence or Run—three or more cards of the same suit.

Speculator—a player who picks up a discard because it matches another card in their hand, even though it does not make a spread.\o

Spread—a group of three or four cards of the same denomination or a sequence of three or more cards of the same suit

Upcard—the card that is turned up after both players are dealt ten cards. In Oklahoma gin it determines the value that you can knock for.

PRODUCER

Bill Pugsley, the driving force behind the writing of this book. Bill saw the need for such a "how to" manual and pressed me into its production.

ANECDOTES

After playing for many years at my neighbor's jewelry store, I had beaten my landlord, Sonny Martini, and a longshoreman, Paul Stallone, plus the watchmaker, Isidore "Janzy" Jansburg so many times that they would not play me anymore.

They began to find other gin players around the city and in Houston who had some major bucks and were willing to gamble. Then they would bet on me so they could recoup some of their losses.

I spent more time playing gin than I did styling hair. I made a lot of money for all of us until we ran out of customers.

Today, as I reflect on those people, I realize they were all bald! I couldn't have gotten their money any other way.

Larry Yeager, the *bookie*. He and I attended the same high school and were acquaintances. Being a bookie he had lots of free time and he would come to my beauty salon, after hours, where we could play without interruption. We must have played over ten thousand games

—150 points, straight gin—over a two-year period.

He was doing very well in his business and he didn't mind me downloading some of his holdings. I also booked bets in my salon for him from my Houston connections. When I moved from downtown Galveston, our games ceased. *Sigh* . . .

Buddy Garcia, the boxer, was at one time the tenth-ranked lightweight in the world. He fought the world champion, Willie Pep, in Madison Square Garden, New York City. Great fighter, Buddy, but a lousy gin player. Too many punches made him think "funny."

And Lord, how he cheated. That made up 90% of our games. I learned more about cheating from this man than all others combined. And I beat him to a pulp, just as Willie Pep did. Well, that is not completely true. He was beating Pep in the first round and Pep hit him below the belt AFTER the bell and Buddy couldn't answer the bell for the next round. That's how Buddy learned to cheat, the hard way.

Stan Schreiber, the social misfit, is a genius in every respect. He spent five years being entertained by me when he became ill and couldn't work. We played gin for a couple of hours every day. We must have played 15,000 games at a dollar a game and if I won more than one hundred dollars from him it would be a great victory; he is one incredible player.

The one person I would rather play on the *internet* and not in person is Les "Flip" Berry, the son of one of my best friends. He is a magician, very adept with cards and coins.

When playing him I have to count the cards after every hand or he will annihilate me. Don't ever play gin with a sleight-of-hand artist.

Aaron Schneider, my absolute *best* friend, is the one player I cannot intimidate. We never play for money, just aggravation. He got so accustomed to losing to me that it didn't bother him at all, so he finally started winning. Now, sometimes, it bothers me (but not that much).

Actually, Aaron's game improved by playing me. He'll pick up anything I discard. Hell, he will even pick up a hot stove! But, he is fun to play, since I always play him in my *relaxed* mode.

Another character of longevity in the gin playing arena is a lady named Irene Ayers, who was a regular Monday client. While she sat under the dryer, we would play gin. At least I was playing gin. To this day I don't know what she was doing. During the forty-two years we played, which covered a span of 6,552 games, she won two of them; August of 1957 and March of 1991. I remember because I had to do her hair for free if she ever won. I'll have to say this, she was a good sport and a gracious loser.

Probably the worst player I've ever played in person is Bill Pugsley; the person directly responsible for me writing this book. I would like to stand behind him some day and watch him play so I could find out what the hell he is thinking. He, too, is a magician. He makes good *hands* disappear. I think he wanted me to write this book so he can learn how to play correctly.

After playing on the *internet* (mostly on World Play Gin) for the past six months, I have played over 2,000 games and have won 75% of them. But *winning* is not the largest reward for playing, making new friends is. It has been a wonderful experience and I'm looking forward to meeting more players.

Gin on the *internet* is a lot of fun and there are always players available. Tournaments are run daily by some fun-type people. It's an experience that I would recommend to everyone who likes to play gin against formidable opponents.

QUOTES

The most expensive gin lessons have come across the table from Charles Killebrew. Thirty years of lessons and I have yet to beat him.

John Winslow
Dallas, TX

I have cherished Charley Killebrew's friendship for 50 years, and I have yet to best him at gin rummy . . . he's the greatest!

Stan Schreiber
Dallas, TX

#1, CKILL2015—All I can say is, "Man . . . does this guy have a future as a gin player or what?" He has impressed the editors (World Play Gin) as few others have. This man is someone to be reckoned with.

Let me mention an online name to you, CKILL2015. Do you recognize it? Are you aware who he is? If not you've been stuck in a hole somewhere because Chuck is definitely the finest gin player on line.

Flairman99
New York, NY

Ich wundere mich auf sein gin rummy genau so schlecht is wie sein tennis.

Eddie Marx
Cologne, Germany

If he was as good as he thinks he is, he would have never lost a game in his life! But he wrote this book, so I guess that makes him an expert. All he does is aggravate you to death . . . and then usually wins. He's my best friend. I love him.

Aaron Schneider
Houston, TX

Having spent the last several years of my life learning the intricacies of card manipulation and sleight of hand magic, I can say with almost 50/50 certainty that the overwhelming win-loss record amassed by Charley may not have involved much cheating.

Les "Flip" Berry
Atlanta, GA

He cheats! I can't prove it, but I know he cheats and I won't play him!

Sue Berry
Columbus, MS

I've never played Charley in gin rummy but if he plays gin as well as he plays bridge, he should win the majority of his games.

F. Paul Head
Bridge Partner
Galveston, TX

Charley is an "elegant" gin player. Probably the most gracious part of knowing Charley is he has been more than willing to teach me personally how to become a better gin player by pointing out my mistakes in our private games. When playing him, if you pay attention, you cannot help but become a better player.

Eve Meyer
North Glen, CA

Charley's willingness to share with the card community is something no one should pass on. I recommend serious players read and learn the nuances of the game from a player who knows a lot about winning. I will be the first in line when his book is published.

L. Berry
Columbus, MS

Charley has been a winner at every undertaking in his entire life. That's why I chose him to be my campaign manager. And, I won!

Roger "Bo" Quiroga,
Mayor of Galveston, TX

ABOUT THE AUTHOR

Born October 21, 1931, on the Island of Galveston off the coast of Texas, where gambling was rampant during his developing years. Gambling was a way of life in Galveston until 1957 when it was finally shut down. Well, almost.

Charley Killebrew, Author

There were many card players to compete with and almost always for money. There were places to go just to play hearts, poker, boure' (booray), bridge, blackjack, cribbage and gin rummy.

Gin was the most popular because it only required two players, and you depended only upon yourself to be victorious! Unlike sitting in a poker, boure, or blackjack, games that required four or more players, or bridge, where you needed a partner, gin could be played anywhere, any time.

Charley Killebrew was educated at Catholic schools in Galveston from kindergarten through the University of St. Thomas in nearby Houston. Monies were always raised in catholic schools through raffles, bingo, tip-books and other forms of gambling, so it seemed only natural that these types of activities must be moral, otherwise the good priests and nuns wouldn't have condoned it.

Plus, the bishop of the diocese, who Charley served mass for at his chapel, was always encouraging him to help raise money for the catholic charities.

Charley started playing gin at the age of five with his father and his siblings. By the time he reached sixteen, he was playing local well-known gamblers for pocket money. He also spent a considerable amount of time as a pool hustler, playing "fourteen-one (straight pool)" and nine-ball, but after marrying gave up those night-time activities in favor of a more congenial home life.

During the Korean conflict while in the Marine Corps, there was ample time for card playing and he enjoyed an enormous amount of success. Later, working as a hairstylist in downtown Galveston, he played gin at his neighbor's jewelry store during the day and his own establishment at night and amassed some impressive winnings.

Because of his reputation, players came from all over town and from other towns, to *get some action* and knock the king off his throne; it never happened.

You don't have to come to Galveston to play gin against Charley Killebrew, challenge him on the net. World Play Gin. Look for CKill2015. Just be ready to get your butt kicked!